D0435463

Barely
Composed

Barely
Composed

Poems

Alice Fulton

W. W. Norton & Company
New York • London

For information about permission to reproduce selections from this book,
write to Permissions, W. W. Norton & Company, Inc.,
500 Fifth Avenue, New York, NY 10110

For information about special discounts for bulk purchases,
please contact W. W. Norton Special Sales at
specialsales@wwnorton.com or 800-233-4830

Manufacturing by Courier Westford
Book design by Molly Heron
Production managers: Devon Zahn and Ruth Toda

ISBN 978-0-393-24488-5

W. W. Norton & Company, Inc.
500 Fifth Avenue, New York, N.Y. 10110
www.wwnorton.com

W. W. Norton & Company Ltd.
Castle House, 75/76 Wells Street, London W1T 3QT

1 2 3 4 5 6 7 8 9 0

for
　　Hank

and
　　in memory of my mother,
　　Mary Callahan Fulton

Contents

IV

V

Barely
Composed

Because We Never Practiced
   With The Escape Chamber

we had to read the instructions as we sank.
In a hand like carded lace. *Not nuclear warheads*
on the sea's floor nor the violet glow over the reactor
will outlive this sorrowful rhyme. Vain halo! My project
becalmed, I'll find I've built a monument
more passing than a breeze. It will cost us,
Pobrecito. We can't buy a prayer. Did you call
my name or was that the floorboard
wheezing? These memories won't get any bigger,
will they? I think something is coming that will
vastly improve our quietude. I'm growing
snow crystals from vapor in anticipation and praying
for the velvet-cushioned kneeler that I need to pray.
I made this little sound for you to wait in.

The Next Big Thing

I know I cannot tell it all forever and so I want to tell it

all of you, a sparkscale audible from the corner of

my ear, visible if I look just to the side of
where you are. If I surface as I move from
seclusion to seclusion, trusting the attitude
gyroscope to finesse the pitch and roll, the control

moment gyroscope to secure my hold.
I feel free as water fangling over stone and falling

with a dazzle on the next big thing, presence
ribboned up in ink, instant and constant,

all tied up in gift. Just wrap the world
around a pen and draw a cradle in a lake
and in the cradle draw a flywheel
free from mortal rust. I saw a skunk
just puttering around the yard
on a day like this.
                    No bigs.

The carriage jogs on the vintage
Hermes with its gunked up keys
and done black ribbon. The escapement

allows travel. No need to fix creation
with wire at the base. If a cascade exists just to be

riveting, if that is why a gyroscope exists. To be

a thing-of-beauty-toy-forever kind of

thing. Have you seen it levitate
on point and sideways like
some android ballerina? While an airy armature
coddles its serenity. It must be pleasing to bow a little

as you pivot and have your way with space.
To roll the world around a pen

to invent a center. Then forget the pen.
The Carriage held but just Ourselves—

its motion sprightly, tilting side to
side, while the axle spun so fast it looked so still.
To keep the god fan going. These sketches testify
to collapsing arrangements
whose underlying edifice is time. Mercury wings
on our double-
                              knotted sneakers,

a white satin bow on the coachman's whip.

Claustrophilia

It's just me throwing myself at you,
romance as usual, us times us,

not lust but moxibustion,
a substance burning close

to the body as possible
without risk of immolation.

Nearness without contact
causes numbness. Analgesia.

Pins and needles. As the snugness
of the surgeon's glove causes hand fatigue.

At least this procedure
requires no swag or goody bags,

stuff bestowed upon the stars
at their luxe functions.

There's no dress code,
though leg irons

are always appropriate.
And if anyone says what the hell

are you wearing in Esperanto
—*Kion diable vi portas?*—

tell them anguish
is the universal language.

Stars turn to trainwrecks
and my heart goes out

admirers gush. Ground to a velvet!
But never mind the downside,

mon semblable, mon crush.
Love is just the retaliation of light.

It is so profligate, you know,
so rich with rush.

Triptych For Topological Heart

It befalls us. An exchanged glance, reflective spasm.

Is it a fantastically unlaminated question set in flesh
or valentine that wears the air as its apparel?
If you cut a heart from parchment, is it still
a heart? A nontrivial knot, where turns of every gradient
may kiss and tell. Does the vessel have edges?
Or is it all connectedness, an embedding to be stretched
or bent. Imagine being simultaneously alive,
bound in both directions with a bow! Is it diachronic,
a phenomenon that changes over time? Without ardor,
theory suffers. That's why I'm stuck on you with wanton glue, per-
severing, styling something blobbish and macabre
into something pointed, neat. Love is a gift
that springs from an unlit spot. Resin and rue.
Even when I'm in the dark I'm in the dark with you.

Say it quivers rather than contracts, fluttery with ruptions.

Doctors call it holiday heart. Valentine's Day—
named for a saint whose head is venerated in Rome—
is also National Organ Donor Day, okay?
Give anatomical dark chocolates infused with true
invariance. With smoked salt pepper and beau-
jolais in a plain brown box embellished with praises
in a romance language in your hand. Please
none cosseted in plush like the stuff inside
a coffin. I'm just praying. Can you find a pulse
or dry needle trigger point? Just saying
this fudge has tears in it. Someone's been sweating
over this. Listen, Mr. Stethoscope, I'm at the end
of my hope. Still I'll grow another
blossom for that blossom-crowned skull.

Some give vinegar valentines. No pillow words.

Just floppy organ thistleburr. Froot Loops and craft
wire fashioned on a snarky jig: "To My Pocket Prince."
"By Bitch Possessed." Tough tits, isn't it? Some call it a day
marked by commodified flowers, obligation chocolate.
Some live on clinical sprinkles, asking where's the feast.
The carnelian pin with openwork components
that let you see its self-pleasuring mechanism, storm
hormones, and single pulsing vein. What even is it?
Here's the thing. A gift cannot be cynical
unless the giver is. I will pay you to test this
for me. Its closets vast with steadfastness at best
at least for me surpass all other closets in the flesh.
I'm sending this from my memory foam head.
Valentines intensify the surface, heart the depths.

After The Angelectomy

And where my organ of veneration should be—
wormwood and gall. Grudge sliver.

Wailbone, iron, bitters. I mean to say the miniature
waterfalls have all dried up in this miniature

place where day is duty cubed, time is time on task
and every mind optimized for compliance.

Time to delint my black denim traveling stuff.
The fluorescent major highlighter has dimmed

to minor. I'm so dying I wrote
when I meant to write so tired.

And when I sleep I dream only that
I'm sleeping. Please see my black stuff's

dusted off. Night has no dilution anxieties,
but only the infinites are happy:

Math. Time. Everything happy goes
to many decimal places

while flesh passes through
gradations of glory. I visualized it,

the nurse said of the bedsore. Everything exists
at the courtesy of everything else.

Please see that my grave is kept clean.
Beloveds, finite things

in which the infinite endangered itself,
excarnate to memory and the divine substance

has limited liability. You're kind,
I tell the infinite. Too kind.

Wow Moment

From the guts of the house, I hear my mother crying
for her mother and wish I understood
the principles of tranquillity. How to rest

the mind on a likeness of a blast furnace
framed in formica by anon. A photo of lounge
chairs with folded tartan lap robes. An untitled typology of

industrial parks. The gentle interface of yawn and nature.
It would soothe us. It would soothe us. We would be soothed
by that slow looking with a limited truth value. See

how the realtor's lens makes everything look larger
and there's so much glare the floor looks wow
under the smartificial xmas tree.

After studying Comparative Reality
I began *Die Polyvinylchloride Tannenbaumserie*.
Turn off that tiny tasteful star, I commanded.

While you're alive there's no time
for minor amazements. Turn off the sallow pages of
your paralegal pad. I don't need a light to think

of you. I don't need a god to pray.
Some things are glow alone. I said one thing you said
you remembered I said. Was it will you be my

trophy friend? Or are you someone else's
difficult person? I mean the more myself I
become the less intelligible I seem to others.

I know what you mean you said.
It's like the time I was hired to speak
on hedonism to the monks and nuns.

Did I say most religion is devotional
expediency? Or religion doesn't worry about being
religious, its wisdom corrupted by its brilliance as light

passing near the sun is deflected
in its path. Deep in its caprices,
the whole body thinks it's understood.

To think otherwise is isolating. When I said
hedonism stressed cheerfulness,
there were disappointed groans. Look, I'm sorry

I gave you an ornament shaped like a hollow look.
I liked its trinket brightness. Just don't give me
a water tower dressed up as a church steeple.

See how those teardrop lights make every object
jump? The memory does. You made me love.
Was it exile in honey is still exile? Am I the fire

or just another flame? Please sell me an indulgence,
I begged a monk. And tell me what creature, what peril,
could craft that sound that night

dropped like a nubile sliver in my ear.
There is no freedom of silence
when morture forces us to speak

from organs other than the heart.
It was something about love. A far cry. It was come to me
unmediated, go to god lengths. In great things,

the attempt alone is sufficient. I think this
'cause I'm finite. That's an understanding
to which reason can only aspire

though an entire speech community labored
for generations to say it in a fair hand clearly
dated and scented with lavender. My one and only only

a crass color orgy will get us through
the dusk ahead, the months gray as donkey.
See how it grows its own cross of fur

and bears it on its back? I showed you that.

II

Forcible Touching

Flaying the blank. The crayon in a death grip, rubbing it in.
This coloring book, the Grief Counselor said, *will help. It is a good idea*
      to never tell the child
        the deceased went on a trip. Never tell the child
        the deceased is sleeping. It is a good idea to

not be afraid. While the child colors Once upon a time
there was a happy little chipmunk named Chipper
      who liked to play with his sibling *it is good*
        to say it is normal and even. To stamp out fantasies.

The pound is by the petting zoo.
      My first day, I do chambers,
      the Animal Control guy said,
      and his tongue was unAmerican.

      Push animal in, close door, do switch.
      I hear the gas, shh, shh.

We can hardly stand the wait, the Chipmunks sang in eunuch
harmony. Come on so. Another Lazarus memory,

winkling out of the cave in its graveclothes, vastated
by its visit to oblivion. You have to think of it
all the time because not to think of it means a moment

when the thought returns compounded, shocking as a defibrillator.
The heart. The clacking of that light percussion.

The clicking of beads on the reckoning frame. Abacus,
from dust. Coloring is a kind of bruxism. The gelding ground

his teeth, a rhythmic crunch. My sister was the one
with the beautiful touch. Light hands. The voice of the shuttle ==

as on a clumsy native loom she wove a brilliant fabric,
working words in red. *When the child colors* One day
       Chipper's mom told him his sibling
       had died *it is all right*
       to suggest crayons for the blotchy insides
       of the ears the blank circles in the eyes
       that indicate reflection. Unmellow Yell-
       ow Cool and Crazy Blue. The Animal Control

guy trembled in the one tongue
       that must do for all his days. *I hear animal soundings.*

       Cage cage scream scream. So pain.
       In this point I scared. I sad

       I'm gonna lose job here after.
       I was just pray to God. Sad you God

       help them die quick, sad hour
       farther. Dwell upon it always

or there'll be a whipflash, a concussed return.
I pushed the snaffle into his plush.
He was carrying good flesh. The voice of the shuttle is classic

tabloid stuff. Say her brother-in-law raped her
and cut out her tongue. How with shaking hands
she gathered up her tender vittles and comforters.
How there's a fund of talent in distress
and misery learns cunning.

When children color When someone dies
their heart and brain stop beating and
      thinking someone dead cannot speak
      cry laugh or eat *children may think something.*
      They might even feel == *Granny Smith*
      Screamin' Green Hot Pink.

Call Animal Control. *Sad you God*
      kill animals faster, hollow be their name.

      But when animals doesn't die quick, I sad
      gosh, gee, what's goin on here, who ideas this?

Long poles with nooses. Jerk it along
while fending it off. Dwell on it always
or there'll be an awful dawning.
Curry with an over and over
oil for glow. The voice of the shuttle
is nectar and ambrosia. She wove her trauma into
a coat and sent it to her sister

who was the rapist's wife. And her sister ghastly
killed their son and cooked and served him
to her rapist spouse for lunch.
If the child colors special people

called Funeral Directors took care
      of Chipper's sibling's body in a pretty house
      called a Funeral Home *over and over*
      it is called Spooking in Place. It is Per-
      severing or Dwelling in the Gate.
Come on so. He tapped his watch

      and time leaked out. Abacus to dust.
      To chambers. So money. It take one minute for unconscience.
      Five minute for heart. For so long. For why?

So the memory won't come back blown up
every hour is that. The brain is beating
not the heart. There seems to be some frost
on the left ventricle. Give, I said and gazed into
the voice of the shuttle == harness and warp.
Selvedge, treadle, beader.

When the rapist learned about his shudder lunch
he chased the sisters and all three were turned to birds.
The gods were the ones with the terrible touch.
When children get frowny coloring When

the Funeral Director took Chipper into a special
      room where his sibling's body was lying in a very special
      box called a Casket *Do not be afraid to say Blizzard*
      Blue Midnight Blue Shadow Blue Surf's Up. Defib-
      rillate. Get rid of myths. Children may think
      something. Concealed in ivy. They made the person die.
      The person will return. It is quite surprising.
      Bound hand and foot with graveclothes!

Ask animal control. *So what you going to do*
      the long death coming? Shoot,
      burn, drown, freeze alive. Electrocute.
      Use decompassion. Needle in heart. So pain!

Think of it always. Not to means a moment
blasting back—shh, shh.
Sometimes I draped a chain over the tongue
as a control. The classics with their talking animals.
The voice of the shuttle == I've heard it
muttered for 15 minutes afterwards.
Praying, they surmised. But they were not. Sure.

If a child draws word bubbles from the Casket
to the Chipmunktown Cemetery *sign*
      it is fibrillating. It is Twilight Spring
      Flesh Rose Dustbite.

Remove hard nubs like fleshbones
from the ears and the bad animal sounds fly back.
They become birds. Hoopoe, swallow, nightingale.

Coloring the grave may initiate a feeling.
If the child presses at the Cemetery
> some special words are said and the casket with the body
> in it is buried in a grave *so hard the crayon breaks*
> *or colors the page all silvery shades*
> *it is Milkshaking. Use clicker training.*
> *It is Granite Gray and Outer Space Gargoyle Gas Smoke Dirt.*
> *Children may resent you later for not being.*
> *They might even feel. There's a hole in the ghost. You will die*
> *and anyone sick will. Even the hospital will die.*

Come on so. The voice of the shuttle is overness.
So many times I've cut out my own tongue. Never tell the child
vividvioletpurplehearttorchredatomictangerine.
When there's a story you cannot speak
you weave. It is too bright to rest your eyes on
but if you contort yourself your shadow will fall
> over it. It is a good idea. It is quite surprising.

Malus Domestica

I've come to dread the obligatory Apple Festival
where we must pledge our fealty
to the strains of folk drone music
by the shores of an impaired lake.

Where former detainees weep to see
children bobbing for apples
with their hands tied behind their backs

and the shepherd in the sheepskin vest cries
"It's even more fun with a boot on your neck!"
We have a saying: nothing is allowed
but that which is allowed is compulsory.

As an apple evaluator, I judge the russeting
and bloom, the starch index at harvest.
Judge is a euphemism for praise.

A sample is handed through a hole.
Sniff, bite, spit. I stroke
the infected and stunted,
those with a hint of worm.

I praise till I'm stupid
from the labor of praising
these wicked apples. Pluton-658:

"has a shelf-life of 12 million years!"
Belly Slap Wehrmacht:
"triples the cyanide of every seed!"
Gulag Snowblower:

"completely hollow, might be an acquired taste!"
I get a lot of emails that say "I've always wanted
to be an apple evaluator."

Once I cherished the oneness
of every apple's blush, knowing
we might never fall
into these forms of flesh again.

Now I envy the bees drowsing in their blossoms,
drunk on the mouthfeel.
For them, there is no distance

between the necessary and the good.
Why do you keep hitting me
when I'm already dead? the detainee asked
at the enhanced interrogation.

He wanted to wipe his eyes on mine,
but I was busy loading my pockets with apples
for the penitential climb.

Sniff, bite, spit. When I offered him
the latest hybrid, he said
we have a saying: giving it away
doesn't make a thing a gift.

A Tongue-Tie Of Vet Wrap

A conforming bandage, twisted to a string.
We'd been toying with the idea

for some time. It clings to itself and comes in bright.
Or a simple piece of hosiery fastened so

the tongue is extended as far as possible,
the root of it flat against the floor.

We wrap the tongue-tie around it,
pull it tight and anchor it with a knot under

the chin that many volunteer to put their finger in.
"Its tongue was chillin' out the side of its mouth like :-P

It was funny and cute." Like us
it carries its tongue against the roof pushing

the saliva back. But tongue tied,
it's like :-|~~~ Well put

your own tongue on the floor. See how long before
but oops you can't because you can't ==

They always resist. Some bite
their tongues, some tongues turn

black from being. Mutilation happens.
I mean just to be near it == proximate

is a slur. At the very least there's a track
the pink of your own exactly.

=========

If ink could melt the page
in restraints == the page stitched with night, a tiny history

in its gob, the choking cloth, toca, while torture music
pounds SOLOUDTHERESTSAREDEMOLISHED.

Some wear ear defenders to increase resistance, reduce
the amplitude. If empathy could squirm through

the space around the ink the final flesh burden
might be determined. But every transparency gives

onto an opacity, the white muck beneath
the utterance hysterically faint, the voices ray-

gunned, bush-
whacked, their histories baled

with soft annealed mechanic's wire. Haywire.
Fascists worship what is strong,

mystics what is weak. A voice stuttering
through an operculum == hard flap.

Just to be near it == in propinquity,
is a taint. The page under

the == the
page in restraints, starved, a famine under wraps,

its negative space headthrobbingly bright.
Revelator, if my voice shrinks

to a whisper say say it
in plain American which

cats and dogs can read. Say say it
in Swiss Army Knife. It will cure your throat ache.

Say ink is the black salve, the bride ==
though it feels clumsy, though you feel

you're writing with an extremity other
than the hand. The tongue. Though I feel

this history will never end,
that when I look through a transparency I'll see

another transparency. A window that gives
onto a mandala of bright funneled backbreakingly

between tiny raised lines.
It flaps, an operculum. It blazes and spins, depending.

Every inch of it exists in relation
so it's hard to grasp

the scale. When the lining, the space
under the == is tattooed

with transparent ink. Beholder, be sparkscript,
object of ignition. Say you must flame

through that restriction or who will who will
story the horror, if not you? The sub-

merged == rosa == lingual == dermal == versive.
The emptiness there

not there. With this biro, bic, pixel.
With this papermate. I thee.

Reckoning Frame

Tell the truth. █████ rage but never force. Go █ and in █ and.
████████████████ o is the widest word ████████
██████ . . . pull it tight and anchor it with a █ not ██████
██ . A █ forming █ andage, twisted to a st █ ing. Not even vet
wrap █ ██████ laced ██ in the dark ████████████ . . . a
corset █ ice, █ ouchsafed with stays. Or a simple █ i █ ce of hosiery
fastened so █████████████████████████████████
████████████████ the tongue is ex ███ ed as far as possible.
Do not ███████ speak ██ when spoken to in a v █ ice. At a time
like this, it's ████ █████████████ p █ ain why. It is good to have
█ ouching. Let them █ ake some. This █ akes them closer. This
█ akes them feel. This is not █ rue. This is normal and should ██ .
It is o ██ . It is all █████ . Tell the truth. Time █ does us. It has
██████ me ████████████████████████ . It has █ laced me in
████ ██████████████████████ ever force. ████████ the grave
████████ ate feeling. ██████████████████████ . It is ███████████
Ex ████████████████████████████ ink. Do not wear bright anything.
Keep your ███████ ████████ ████████ █████████████ Never ██
████████ █████████████████████████████████████ person
██████████████ laced ██ in the dark ██████████████████ .
This is natural ██████████████ . ████████████████ is is normal and
even. ██ is is ██ rue. It ███ aced me in the dark ███████████████
███████████ its tongue against the █ oof █ ushing the █ aliva back.
█ reeder reactor ████████ , if ██ voice █ inks to a █ isper say
say it. █ now █ is is ███ mal ██ eve █ . Even the ████████ will die.
████████████████████ .

III

Personally Engraved

There are many opportunities here for unrequited friendship,
the offer letter said. All you need is a chain saw and die grinder.

In this spirit I force my eyes across your message,
revisiting that due diligence tone you do so well.

I'm searching for some whispered twist or shout,
but all emotion's leveled, the way a child will draw

a snowman and a mansion the same size.
What is a dedicated icemaker

dedicated to? Do you really think
those shades you wear above your head

will keep the sun out of your mind?
Rainbows stick to any abject object.

That's why I'm wearing that same old funky dress.
When you kissed my forehead it felt like the priest's

thumbscrew touch rubbing in the dust-
thou-art Ash Wednesday smudge.

I've learned the dance instructor's expository gestures.
Now I'm learning tangos to be danced alone.

While comrades buff officious cases
barfed from their brains—

eight parts moon venom one part nose waste—
I ask *can mine be personally engraved?*

I'm living in a please state, smarming
how I've long admired your hardscape of artists

morphed to small appliances. That being said,
I'm having issues. Do you really think

that scarf will keep your snowman warm?

Peroral

It's like a prison that makes itself at home in you,
like so not worth it, so not mattering, and so
fair King of Not, you self-release, secede, sowing
misgivings as you go. You're it, you're all, all
eyes on you, you own this minute, this misdream,
itch, and ache. Want air? Is this where you came in?
Want like *straightforwardness*, *footloose yelp*, *rue*, *am*
I not making myself dear? I'm animate, you know,
if on hold, deterred, deposed. Deflattered.
And you—you're like bye-bye. You judge me
and leave me, but the dreamswerve, regifting,
grows intimate, into what's at stake. Isn't it rich?
Isn't this it? This caustic awakening, as is. As us.
This knot of not mattering, isn't it like enough?

Beaten Into Leaf

You are so not gold.
    So ruffled,
stooping, hunchbacked
    and wishing
to be closer to gold's calm repose.
    Inert and beaten
into leaf, free
    of snits and scolds.
Hammered, recast
    by lost-wax techniques.
Ductilemalleable.
    Reflective yet unflappable.
How great must it be
    to be not
needy? An irrational
    deep magnet
whose lack of reciprocity is valued
    as a lack of rust.
In gold we trust.

We like the way it can be fashioned
    into tiny hives
and worn beneath the skin,
    dispensing medicines.
Or used inside the bodies of those
    who can't fully close their eyes.

Gold implants work
    with gravity
so eyes can close.
    It is a mercy. It is a mercy
to close your eyes,
    you know. You know

gold teeth or plated diaphragm
    domes with mouthpiece
components that transcribe voice
    vibrations into currents
would make you more
    permanent even when exposed
to rain and snow.
    Or you could come equipped
with gold-faced mirrors
    like the ones inside
telescopes that can detect
    a single candle burning on
the surface of the moon.
    Now there's a pretty skill.
Though there is no candle
    burning on the moon,
we marvel still.

They say a trader can protect herself
    with scales or acid.
They say it makes a nice death mask.
    Tears won't change it.

Is that not great?
    Why then do I scruple
to entirely embrace it?
    It is too precious
for small transactions
    and too heavy
for large ones.
    It has nothing to prove.
Paper is its substitute.

Custom Clamshell Cases

This thrashing. This gluttonous.
This at its mercy, clutch to clutch.
This gilt-stamped bombastic.
Red purse stashed in sulk.
This pluckfoam lovely and crypto-
sonar radar room. This telltale.
Ritual implement. Four-chambered
bilge pump. Blind-embossed die-cut.
This gladsome. This tragic.
      That likes a minor carnival.
A snow day's cancellations.
A sand mandala with time in its gut
it loves. A mandala that gyroscopes
about its lotus compass
till its design is swept,
its energy left elsewhere.
A bliss that lives
by direct transmission
without being in any way
      diminished. It likes
an emptiness with nothing devious
but much that's secretive
about it. That doesn't suffer
and cannot be depleted.
That isn't made of time is why.
And envies any emanation body

whose carnival is optional
rather than perforce.
          This offal. This roarious.
At the end we sweep its design and place
its energy elsewhere. "It's the first piece of
equipment we remove and it's always
a bloody mess. This grubby,
this lumpen," the ferryman cried
as he performed a granular sort
of the ephemera consigned him.

A Thinkable Rampage

Self-glittering,
      free   from light amazespace!
                                Full
                                of reflection, it lets me
           see what's on the surface when I'm well

                below the waves.
      I
could forget it's there, except it keeps re-   minding me.
                            Your periscope
             has a very kind eye said
             an ultraviolet soul with ultraviolet
                        sight.
Sometimes it darkens rather than self-glows.

Gets tired. Of predicting.
      Witnessing. "The rest
      next time."   It is
             next time. Gone anguish,
                I reproach
                a world
             in which my protest stands
             alone.
On a thinkable rampage, on a tear, I grow my passions into
a candle.
         When I can

do that why do
anything
else?
When it says I made a right dog's dinner of things it's on vacation
brain.

Don't sweat it. Though as Jesus once told me, sweat is

the smell of sanctity.
Then   he unplugged the cooling unit
that pumped
subzero through
my moves and my passions

grew me
into
a candle. When they can do that why do any-   thing else?
We came to
pick your brains,
they said and I squeamed.
We're going to
regurgitate you is the only worse expression.

Interred diary, its hurt surface
still, still
it suffers without shudders   trussed in skull
the clamor of thinking
how
many times

                    an idea hammered
                    to a fineness will bind the earth.
            Long ago some thought thought
            sprang from the heart so
                    noisy buoyant—

not from the brain so
gem
in a shell. And wreathed
in greeny flowers that grow beside the Styx—not never laurels
                                    those only flowers whose

        name I can't recall—I'll think of it.

Postscript.
        Oracle,   I'll kiss your chapped lips.
                                        You who were
                                        invented so
                time could say this.

Black Salve

The parts are more articulate than the whole,
chattier, if abject, their usefulness stupified.
They call it learning the iron, this stripping
the sheath to what's beneath,
the wheels and screws in a gelded heap.
Vile hierarchies == humans above humans above
animals == are vivisected at three a.m.
when the head becomes a pressure hull.
Exdreams fester in that nave of night
they call the dead. While the minute-
hand limps forward, bowing to each moment,
its rhythm stately as a wedding party's
leaden step. Learning the iron! All duration ends
in a devouring. Eternity, the word, is like a lace
handkerchief waving down a train.
I keep taking things apart
to find what makes them froth,
and sleep with my watch on,
a tiny hand stirring a tiny boiling pot.

Personal Reactor

The protogeegaws of the new world
had long been glossed with drool.

High acid saliva made it hard for us
to form and maintain our shells.
I was retooled, my flesh turned to things
of which I was anxious
that you should engross at least half.
Periscopeglandssnorkelinductionmast
ventilationexhaustlinesternplanes
activatorrudderram. I wanted to be neither
heavier nor lighter than whatever
I displaced. The variable ballast

tank compensated as the climate waxed
warmer, sadder, dumber.
And the ocean, absorbing bad
from air, acidified. Its subjugation was
the office of each watchful companion,
each component clunky with numbers:
plutonbilgepumpsinglewarheadmissile.
The reactor was heaviest, a black mass
in its cosseted capsule, its lining finer
than its outside. Monstrous fine,
an omniofficious l'awful
thermos thing. Liquid metal
or pure water cooled the core.

I could not express my abhorrence
in the surfaced or submerged condition.
Crydrops! My Astonishment, the pressure
in the machine was set too high,
the technician's eye cold as tile. The tormenta
was so calm on top, so uranium oxide
drilled into pins sealed inside cladding
arranged in bundles underneath!
It was not composure but containment.
A stout grind of all works
optimized for compliance

and mutilated by scruples, my mind

turned to a conscience of which I was dying
for you to disarm just half.

Like sailors dozing on a bed of torpedoes, we sleep
and our elastic sleep mask stretches

over everything. We dream far reaching.
It is being alive that keeps us incomplete.
My Solitude, the lining is much finer
than the outside. It has such pulchritude.
Sepulchral. It has that mouth feel. Tendersalt. The sea

turned to rubble covered with weeds.
We grind its bones to make our bread.
The corals grow pale
with essential fatigue, sea turtles morph
to amuse-bouches in the mega-hotels.
Crown-of-thorn starfish, mass bleaching
events—spare me the details. Only silence boasts

neutral buoyancy, neither heavier nor lighter
than what it displaces, the protogeegaws
of the new world glossed with lust.
If only they could sense
their own prodigious dullness. As the hush
grows heavy with vanquished

citations, the accommodation of
debts, time grinds our bones to make its bed.
We're sullied putty in such hands.
Won't you condole? When you probe
my solitude there could be none

so monopolized by ecstasy as I.

Phenylbutazone might deflame me
but my page reminds me to conclude.

⇒⇐

"As you set out for Ithaca, hope the voyage is a long one."
I'll get there by full-body prostrations

collecting dedications on the way:
For Blub with conjugal love.
For all the Robots I have lied to.
For the Pet who loves me best.
For the Virgin of the Unsheltered.
If you could know my solitude there could be none

so colonized by quietude as I. My self
would turn to an ocean of which I am certain
you would engross at least half.
I'd throw off my standard issue
foulweather and venerate the snow
trapped in your eyelashes. I'd donate my leg irons.
Do children still make those chains of bright

construction paper? Rags and ink.
Though time will hazard this narration
bearing in its outstretched hour
my own climacteric when everything suddens
at once, I remain a mind awakened
by a reasonable exertion, imagining the world
will catch each syllable with panting eagerness anxious

for that preferment of which at present
there seems not the slightest chance.

And introducing excess into schemes of such
composure, the silence grows

audible, glossing a greater silence

and conveying with its amplitude
our own names lit in reticence.

IV

Sidereal Elegy

Time is in the details. Someone had to tell Polaris
      it would not always be
the pole star. That important standard candle
though it was, eventually, vast ages hence,
      earth's fickle axis would fix
upon another. Someday Vega would replace it,
      though we would not name names.
Meanwhile, revolutions. Meanwhile, stalined
or styxed. Nightly we prayed for inertial guidance.
      We lay awake thinking time itself would cry
to see the century it compiled, but all its gears
and mechanisms were sealed. The "Mists of Time,"
      stapled between scare quotes! *Come to me,*
they whispered, and even the stars obeyed.

Still World Nocturne

Listen, only night is watching the night nurse,
and her smoker's voice is not a voice I trust.

Yet I wake up and the world's still here—a blur

of how to speak or dress—which words or skirt
or pair of powdered, tear-resistant gloves.

Sisters, only night is watching the night nurse,

and no matter what we've heard, she's heard much worse—
the vacuum's roar, our mother crying Mother!

and asking if the world's still here—while versed

in flawed priorities, I numbly parse
a sweat of student essays, changing *is* to *was*.

Children, only night is watching the night nurse.

Tomorrow we'll confess all our concerns
about that villanelle's dumb rhymes on love.

We'll wake up to the world that's here—a burr

of sun stuck to a catheter's gold purse,
queasy music, wicked drugs. Still Mother,

only night will watch as I, the night nurse,

wake up to a world unhere, unyours.

Mahamudra Elegy

Then emptiness grew more empty,
the scent of scentlessness.
          How could it be?
When emptiness is that which can't be

emptied any more, neither malicious nor
          a state that welcomes us
with munificent alohas.
I fingered it like an incision, fondled it

          like a rosary of thorns, thinking
if every instant holds
the maximum abridged, tranquillity must be
          somewhere in the mix. So concentrate.

A live volcano is the recommended site
for certain meditations. Think time
          exists because a dropped glass
breaks and here we are existing,

witnessing the ornaments,
          decorative yet dear. Mundanities
that dazzling seem extruded by a star.
          Stellifactions. Mahamudra.

Words to conjure with. The great
seal, great gesture, the mahamudra
          holds snowflakes to their certitudes of lace.
While fire thinks fire

is what everything aspires to, time thinks
          through its helpless locks: its ambergris
flocked with a sailor's buttons, its mud wasp
buzzing like a mini vac. Every solid is a clock.

Active Night

Time broke out in blue-violet flames, a farm of the eternal
and the suicide prevention fest was cancelled
'cause of rain. It's a sun heavy industry.
They talk and normalize, say the weather is temporary
and it's important for the temporary to be there

so call us if it feels rough. If it feels
sensitive or high. If your spirit compartment, exposed
beyond permissible limits, lies awake singing
come sleep, komsomal, and what have they done
to the rain all night. If you need a sober companion.

They say the temporary won't always fit
as well as the permanent but the temporary serves
an important purpose. It protects the exposed
who long to cease upon the midnight
with no pain, extinguished

by that which they were nourished by
with equipment readied for the purpose in advance.
Who feel their gorge rise, thinking
the chance to be decent was always
before us yet we composed our macht nicht

reports, ordered slaughter from room service,
yumfangen with nitrate-based energy sauce.

We lost track of the particulate, vaunted
without ceasing, our grubcreed like a fire
always looking for a chance to rise. Surely

this mist will stretch like a disposable glove
over the land all the days of our lives
but will it maintain barrier integrity?
While a fell rain falls and unter- and uber-
menschen break out in blue-violent flames

will the temporary overwinter?
Yes, the chance to seize upon the midnight is always
before us, but can we make it live? Can we say
nice twilight glove, make me
an instrument of your collision, your give?

Roar Shock

Many see a flutterby when they look into this

omniscience she sees as a skinniness too densely drawn
or a mystery unhinged by its own symmetry, a twinning
she thinks of as a listener that thinks along
with *she*, fused in a tweed, a red herring-
bone weave in the dazzling darkness
and bleached afterness some see

as a necklace of brilliants curved in gift. As if!

A color visible only in ultra-
violet light or a source beyond mathematics she thinks
of as a second self, an underhum. Or thought. Till she saw
innocence tortured by a force
beyond kindness, an unconditional indifference or

wick for wickedness that wanted trauma dolls.

She tells this as a clock tells time but telling can't diminish it

as clocks can't dwindle time. Who will witness
for the witness? Who'll hold
the beholder? Horses kneeling Christmas Eve,
birds that chirp behind a waterfall
are what others see in what she sees
as us delivered up to this chill that searches *she*.

Doha Melt-Down Elegy

We will give the truth teller an anti-suicide smock.
A dusk tunic from some dark satanic mill?

And wake him three times a night
to check that's he's alive. Because he did not cease

from mental fight nor did his sword sleep
in his hand? He will not be eased. He will be boiled

and handled with boiled gloves, flayed and stretched
flat on a hoop called a writhe? And if a drop of bile

falls on the *why* we will cover it with a needle-
work of starry stripes. And the Immortalization

Committee will embalm it? And God will toss the sky
like a drop cloth over heaven to protect it.

$\Longrightarrow\Longleftarrow$

"This is my fault, isn't it?" the night nurse said
my mother said as she was dying. Did you flip

her every three hours as directed? It doesn't matter
how you are oriented when the future is a room

so small you can sit in the middle and touch
all the walls. When the mind keeps trauma in

an unchanging box. And if a periwinkle flame appears
above the lid the thing is melting down?

If stillness is an encrypted wind

that comes from the night
that never puts off its mourning.

————⟫⟪————

It doesn't matter how fast you are going,
after a thousand full-length prostrations

you will leave a sweat imprint on the ground.
It must be my embodiment fee. The firefly flashing by

the window must be a reflection of the nightlight,
the monk's levitation enabled by an apparatus

underneath his robes. Transparency, a fantasy.
And like a bird that strikes a window and is

stunned by its element gone dense, I fell—

and was given a lesson in the ephemeral
by the cipher of the sky.

＝＜

There is no distance between the necessary and the good,
the revelator said. Was she addressing the seismic

connectedness of things? It was so good—I mean so cold—
my exhalations crystallized and spasmed to arpeggios

when they struck ground. And the wild turkeys suffocated,
their nostrils iced by their own breath.

Truth awakener! Were you saying the necessary
and the good are like prisoners in punitive proximity,

held upright by each other's suffering?
Or if the necessary isn't good it isn't

necessary? Would you just replace this
lavish gulag with a white conch shell?

＝＜

I will now perform miracles to disturb you, time said
as it replaced my mother's voice with an instrument

fashioned from an ascending aorta. Why am I still crying?
You're standing in an elegy gust

that comes from the past. It is heavier, more militant
than innocent wind. Compassion infiltrated by iron

turns rancid. Sanctimonious. It says your sword slept
in your hand. It says you drank an anti-nectar.

I work this cud, too stupid
and struck numb to beg. This grief abscess

no degree of speech can drain, no
tongue, my cud of ugh.

≫≪

It was a good book to be lost with. I began taking notes
and by the end I realized I'd transcribed every line.

It doesn't matter where you are
when the magnetite in your nose provides data

for celestial navigation. It was written in the twilight
language, a script without a dictionary that is

another way of knowing. Another mind that is
a reverie of light? A provenance of. A super-

luminal == above == beside == vibration flashing
through the threshold magnitude.

―――

Only saints who choose their own privations
are free to leave them. We will not be eased.

When her tongue dumbfoundered she stopped
calling for her mother and the night urka

said mouth care will be especially important now.
Night Terror, how will I know when death is near?

Buy q-tips topped with tiny clown-hair-
colored sponges. Stick the especial

nipple in her mouth. For a few seconds.
Whenever. You remember. At first

her lips clasped with especial thirst. You'll know
by its Kremlin complexion, the truth teller said.

―――

As the night nurse lullabies the night,
I might have soothed her.

Melt gummy bears in boiling water
and drink. Because they're dense with glycerin,

a yummy vocal ease? Sew me into my head,
counterworldly wise. It doesn't matter

when you are == when you are
encysted in that isolator

whipped by memory thorns. Mother,
you are dead! You turned into eternity

before my eyes. And I am still extant, living
in a stillness sent by overness.

≫≪

I've heard that from darkness
the mind can gestate halos

made of interred glow. I've heard she dissolved
into those rays and those rays dissolved

into the body of my mind, my brain.
But you won't find her anywhere

unless you put her there yourself, the revelator said.
Remembering is disheveling. God,

why do you need us to die? I asked,
quoting the floatery spasms

of the prayer flags, breeding novenas,
exhorting the afterhere.

As prayer flags give their prayers to wind,
let my constancy compound. As fire metastasizes.

Sew me into my dark
and if a spark falls on my collar, cover it

with a needlework of charnel flowers.
It doesn't matter where I am == it doesn't matter

when I am == it doesn't matter
how fast I am going or how

I am oriented == I will think of her

always and never defer my mourning.
I will sieve the ether for her she is so nearly here.

V

"Make It New"

I find it helpful to imagine writing in a blizzard
    with every inscription

designed to prevent snow
      crystals from drifting in.

It's the opposite of making love to drudgery,
what I do for a dying.

Remove the bitter sediment
trapped in the brewer. Avoid the hive mind.

Go fly a kite, raise a stained glass
window in the sky. It will be new

whether you make it new
or not. It will be full of neo-

shadows. Of *then*—both past and next,
iridescent with suspense. Remember

    time is not the treasure revealer.
More a midge larva creeping

through a waterfall releasing
suction feet. The curiosity rover

lands on Mars! New
breaks the reckoning frame and rests

in pieces. Let me collect its DNA
from the tears on your desk.

A Lightenment On New Year's Eve

Season of no weedwhackers and wind
that moans like a folding choir.
Tonight the old is laid away in smoke.
Tonight the sodality of fire.
        Newness is intensely memorable. It's called
the primacy effect. The Rinpoche of Firstness
is ready for this attentional task. To write
the year's grievances by hand on scrap.
Approach. Feed the burning bowl.
While silence falls, a hybrid of snow.
Rise and kneel. This burning is private.
We're here to get present, gentle memory,

put the past to sleep. Since she enjoys her long night's
festival let me. Some use their digital fireworks
setting to preserve the letting go.
A little bone-like object

marks the distance we must keep.

        ≥≤

Uranium burns with a spectral a peri-
winkle a newclear nukeyouler—
some can't get their mouths around it—flame.
Some experience a gut flutter. How can it be

tranquilized? *Change the world,* the pyropathologist
says without a beat. *Fire has a sense of entitlement.*
It owns the stage. If you do fire
it does you back more deeply. If you do love—
but I was saying. To fire it's all to the tooth.
It's a felony-friendly entity not a force
with whom it is advisable to link your fate.
Thrashglutton candelabra. Flashing ruffian

point bucket. In mind I burn
cremation with its ghastly dairy sound.
Burn some fatuous platitudes:
Whatdoesntkillyoumakesyoustrongitsallgooditsnot

aboutyouattheendofthedaythatbeingsaid
closureclosureclosure—I write *uranium*, *plutonium*
and lower the control rods by hand.
I relinquish these to your fortunes, which promise
to be different from mine, I tell the fire.

⇒⇐

After the offering, we compose letters
of intention for the year ahead:
May I take it or leave it. May I be

pleased to meet you. May I be
in the same boat. May I be
too kind. May I run the risk. May I be

all of a piece. May my
            protective rubber mask not melt. May I
remain to be seen. If I break
these vows, I'll party hard in all that
I renounced. *It's called the abstinence violation*
effect. Sober companion, it's hard to carnival
in a Business Lit cube that disavows
all bossa nova hustle frug and boogaloo.
A party without a procedural guide-

book's like a faculty club without a tattoo
removal service. True fool, my twice-turned
regalia does need to be retooled.

 ⇒⇐

One gasp and she was rebegot

of nightness nullsense nilthings
which are not. No
parched marble memorates her,
just the living cell. Install strict seals
of rubber and titanium and
build a tome around it.
Nor war's quick fire shall burn
nor trick of the night or acid
eat away at or corrode. Though no
good listener's lurking in the density
that if touched would touch

us back. Though the eraser
grays the paper and silence breaks

the state it names, I'll call this hour
her vigil and her Eve. Though molished
with time and old with all
these bratty fire ribbons tucked inside

my head. Though both knees cracked
from falling to my knees. Still this
attentional task. Grasp the evaporate.
Define. A link is a torch made of cloth
dipped in pitch. The link girl runs ahead
to light the way. Writing is the fire
that burns fire. Every silence quotes
a greater silence. Hushdriven

chandelierium. Kindleweed
ashquill. Clasping recombinant
thornglove. I'll call it summery mix.

Daynight, With Mountains Tied Inside

Chandelier too full of brilliance to be indolent.
      Your prisms enunciate the light
and don't need rain to break it into rainbows.
Snow with six crutches in each crystal.
      Your livery your glitter, your purring
made visible. Only inanimate things can sparkle
without sweat. My spinet, the threat of music
      in its depths and miniature busts of men composers
carved of time on top. The hollow bench

held sheet music. Sing me
      Charm Gets In Your Eyes. I hear you best
when undistracted by your body. In headspace
technology, where flowers are living
      in glass globes, their fragrance vivisected.
Anything that blooms that long
will seem inanimate. Heaven. Grief
      like the sea. Keeps going. Over the same wrought
ground. The whole spent moan. Praise dies

in my throat or in the spooky rift
      between itself and its intended. Like a wish-
bone breaking. The little crutch inside
is not a toy. There is no night asylum.
      A restless bed, a haunt preserve,

a blanket rough as sailcloth. But sing me, was it kind
snow sometimes? With true divided lights and nothing
            flawed about it? If song goes wrong,
be dancerly. Dance me, at what point

does west turn to east as it spins?
            I've never understood. Perspective.
How charm gets to yes. Dance me Exile
and the Queendom, by request.
            It is a ferocious thing
to have your body as your instrument.
Glove over glove, let your dance express
            what I've been creeping like a vein of sweat
through a vastness of.

This tune with mountains tied inside
            and many silent letters
can be read as trackers scan the spaces
between toes and birders read the rustle
            left by birds. As any mammal
in its private purr hole knows,
the little crutch inside
            is not a crutch. More a sort of
steeple. Neither silver to be chased

nor gold to be beaten.
            You were == you are
more than ever like that too.

Noon upon noon,
      you customize this solitude
with spires
that want nothing from me
      and rise with no objective
as everything does when happy.

You Own It

For your birthday, I'm learning to pop champagne corks
with a cossack sword when all you asked for was world peace.
I'm actioning the deliverables to wish you many happy returns

of the ecstasies that are imminent when all you requested
was a contentment so quiet it's inaudible. Remember when
I gave you a robe of black silk that floats and does not rustle?
When all you desired was to turn from what was finished and hard

in the darkness. And when you said I gave you what I wanted
myself I gave you what I didn't want: gift certificates to spas
that wax hearts, a blind date with the inventor of friction.

Today I bring an actual-size sunrise and many glow words
from the inmates of this late-stage civilization who navigate
in your slipstream and to whom you say keep rowing.

When you were born you were placed in a small throne on castors
while the Stop Shopping Choir sang hosannas, a defining
moment. People noticed something nascent about you

that persists in your fondness for the first person primordial.
You own it. You know why voices die in throats

and trees struggle in silence: the deepest trauma cannot
spare a sound. If you meet a mystery you do not disturb it

with little picks and suction things. You say the shape
of happiness is too fine for capture spray, and it is well
to remember the days when plastic boxes snapping shut were all
women had to celebrate. Yet it is not seditious to rebel
against a culture like circus music, so cheerful

we'd need a cadaver tendon to fix it. That's what you say.
You are hard to fathom as a guttering compass that is
neither hush nor howl. I'm thinking of the time

you placed an Aeolian harp in the window, took me
by the notebook and asked me to consider why

turkeys bob their heads when they walk and geese don't
though they both waddle. You watched my ethereality show
and commiserated when they adorned my rival

in a deconsecrated rosary bead bikini and sent her to St. Barts
while I was remaindered to an orange jumpsuit organ-swiping plot.
That century I was betrayed by a dedicated icemaker,
you burned a feather pen to revive me. You tried

my device that prevents accidental workplace nudity, vetted
its magnetic veils, and at Christmas sent fruitcake
privacy filters. Remember when I was dismissed as overness

consultant? How you resigned in solidarity and grew
a sky-colored flower since I could not be satisfied
with the sky itself? You gave me a robe of black silk that floats
and does not rustle and advised me to turn from what was finished

and hard in the darkness. If I critiqued the treasure revealer
you said do not test its softness against your cheek.
Today I raise my glass of wheat grass and atmospheric information

to wish you every beyond of thought in which to consider
all that is majorly good. I won't sing Happy Birthday,
a song so overdetermined it sounds bereaved.

I'll sing of passions that persist in the Elysian Fields.
Though shackled to a boulder at the moment, I'm unpacking
boxes from your last move, wrapping the contents

in recycled fire and presenting them to you
as objects exactly forgotten and largely

what you wanted. I nerve myself for the encounter.

There Are A Few Things I Need To Get

to sleep. A dreamboat of submersible iron,
a sea that rocks, narcotic clock. I need
our feelings to glide and turn in unison, silversides.
Snow gristle, stenciled trees, an ice-breaker
escort—who needs them? Spring's your favorite season.
You like its green lotions. Touched by its soft tissues,
you don't miss the jilted winter. Still,
the figure eight motion of lacing a skate
is soothing. A forever effect. Like everything
you do. I've plunged past my crush depth. I can tell
by the way paint flashes and my protective
rubber mask melts on my face. It's not your doing
I like, it's you. You and your green emollients. Now let us chill.
After we're exchanted, we come all so still.

My Task Now Is To Solve The Bells

They are here to perform. How can I
make them my co-creators, salve
their interruptions of air?
What words will they upstage
with their verdict tapestry? Time needs them,
the way anything large that moves only forward
and cannot stop needs a warning signal.
As a train needs a whistle. The train here sounds annoyed,
but the bells sound patient, as if they are stapling time.
They roll through your thinking saying torn,
torn, until your thinking goes like this:
But I == torn == petually in flux which I thought == torn ==
in a tornpacity of singing more at length.
Their sound is leaden, they are so laden
with torn. If you trace a bell to its source,
you'll find a human trying to trap a magnitude
in bronze. Because a bell's task is to snag:
to holiday or moan. When bells begin,
it's best to collaborate with them, to translate them
as best you can. The translation goes:
Don't get too close, I am time made loud.
There is not enough god to go around.
And what I assume you shall assume.
And there is no peace, no silence, after bells.
The air is too infested by a memory of them.
Their lips screwed long upon the torn.

End Fetish: An Index Of Last Lines

a tiny hand stirring a tiny boiling pot.
a white satin bow on the coachman's whip.
After we're exchanted, we come all so still.
an instrument of your collision, your give?
and bears it on its back? I showed you that.
as everything does when happy.
as us delivered up to this chill that searches *she*.
buzzing like a mini vac. Every solid is a clock.
doesn't make a thing a gift.
from the tears on your desk.
I made this little sound for you to wait in.
I tell the infinite. Too kind.
I will sieve the ether for her she is so nearly here.
of the ephemera consigned him.
our own names lit in reticence.
      over it. It is a good idea. It is quite surprising.
Paper is its substitute.
so rich with rush.
that scarf will keep your snowman warm?
Their lips screwed long upon the torn.
they whispered, and even the stars obeyed.
This knot of not-mattering, isn't it like enough?
thornglove. I'll call it summery mix.
      time could say this.

Valentines intensify the surface, heart the depths.
wake up to a world unhere, unyours.
what you wanted. I nerve myself for the encounter.
with this papermate. I thee.

███████████ .

███████████ .

Notes

"Because We Never Practiced With The Escape Chamber" reinscribes two lines from Shakespeare's Sonnet 55, "Not marble, nor the gilded monuments."

"The Next Big Thing" quotes a line from Emily Dickinson's Poem 479 ("Because I could not stop for Death—")

"Malus Domestica" and "Doha Melt-Down Elegy" briefly allude to Simone Weil's essay "The Distance Between the Necessary and the Good." "Doha Melt-Down Elegy" also riffs on two phrases from William Blake's "Jerusalem."

"A Tongue-Tie Of Vet Wrap" quotes a line from "England" by Marianne Moore.

"Peroral" is composed of recombinant words, prefixes, suffixes, and homonyms from Shakespeare's Sonnet 87, and an anagram of its first line, "Farewell, thou art too dear for my possessing."

"Black Salve" contains a line indebted to Walter Benjamin's *Arcade Project*.

"Personal Reactor" quotes the first line of "Ithaka" by Constantine Cavafy.

"Active Night" quotes and contains a slippage on a phrase from Keats's "Ode to a Nightingale."

"Roar Shock" alters the rhetoric of a line from "Aschenglorie" by Paul Celan: *"Niemand / zeugt / für den Zeugen"* ("No one / bears witness / for the witness").

"A Lightenment On New Year's Eve" repurposes lines from "A Nocturnal upon St. Lucy's Day" by John Donne and quotes a phrase from Shakespeare's Sonnet 55.

"My Task Now Is To Solve The Bells" quotes a line from Walt Whitman's "Song of Myself."

Acknowledgments

The Academy of American Poets Poem-A-Day, online feature: "Roar Shock," a slightly different title and version

The Antioch Review: "Black Salve," "My Task Now Is To Solve The Bells," "Peroral"

The Atlantic: "Mahamudra Elegy," "Sidereal Elegy"

Crazyhorse: "Reckoning Frame"

CURA: "Because We Never Practiced With The Escape Chamber" and "There Are A Few Things I Need To Get To Sleep" under the title "Rondo For Singing Clock"

Fifth Wednesday: "A Tongue-Tie Of Vet Wrap"

The Kenyon Review: "A Lightenment On New Year's Eve"

Little Star: "After The Angelectomy," "Custom Clamshell Cases," "Personal Reactor," "Active Night"

The New Yorker: "Claustrophilia," "Malus Domestica," "The Next Big Thing"

Poetry: "Daynight, With Mountains Tied Inside," "'Make It New,'" "Personally Engraved," "Triptych For Topological Heart," "Wow Moment," "You Own It"

Poetry Review (London): "After The Angelectomy," "Because We Never Practiced With The Escape Chamber" under the title "from Rondo For Singing Clock"

Seattle Review: "Beaten Into Leaf" under the title "Barely Composed"

Smartish Pace: "Still World Nocturne"

The Chronicle of Higher Education, online edition: "After The Angelectomy"

Tin House: "Forcible Touching"

Tongue: "A Thinkable Rampage," "Doha Melt-Down Elegy," "End Fetish: An Index Of Last Lines"

"After The Angelectomy" also appeared in *The Hide and Seek Muse: Annotations of Contemporary American Poetry*, edited by Lisa Russ Spaar, Drunken Boat Media, 2013.

"Beaten Into Leaf" was reprinted as "Barely Composed" on *Huffington Post*.

"Claustrophilia" was anthologized in *Poetry in Medicine*, edited by Michael Salcman, Persea Books, 2014.

"Daynight, With Mountains Tied Inside," "'Make It New,'" "Personally Engraved," "Triptych For Topological Heart," "Wow Moment," and "You Own It" were reprinted on the Poetry International Web (Rotterdam).